May this babe
always know &
very much Jes
us and grow to
love Him, too, from the
from this Child, we pray.
Sue Arnold

11/16/96

A BABY
IS A
BLESSING

Edited by Jill Wolf

Photographs by Koren Trygg

ISBN 0-89954-447-9

Yellow Springs, Ohio 45387
Printed in the U.S.A.

CONTENTS

Babies are bits of stardust blown from the hand of God.

—Larry Barretto

It is a peg big enough on which to hang a hope, for every child born into the world is . . . an ever fresh and radiant possibility.

—Kate Douglas Wiggin

Love's Reward   33

Give a little love to a child, and you get a
great deal back.

—*John Ruskin*

Like a Rose   39

The world has no such flower in any land,
And no such pearl in any gulf the sea,
As any babe on any mother's knee.

—*Algernon Swinburne*

A BLESSING FROM ABOVE

Each child carries his own blessing into the world.

— Proverb

What gift has Providence bestowed on man that is so dear to him as his children?

— Cicero

Babies are bits of stardust blown from the hand of God. Lucky the woman who knows the pangs of birth, for she has held a star.

— Larry Barretto

. . . trailing clouds of glory do we come
From God, who is our home:
Heaven lies about us in our infancy!

—William Wordsworth

Father asked us what was God's
noblest work . . . I said *babies*.

—*Louisa May Alcott*

At the Back of the North Wind

Where did you come from, baby dear?
Out of the everywhere into the here.

Where did you get those eyes so blue?
Out of the sky as I came through.

What makes the light in them sparkle
    and spin?
Some of the starry spikes left in.

Where did you get that little tear?
I found it waiting when I got here.

What makes your forehead so smooth
    and high?
A soft hand stroked it as I went by.

What makes your cheek like a
    warm white rose?
I saw something better than
    anyone knows.

Whence that three-cornered smile
   of bliss?
Three angels gave me at once a kiss.

Where did you get this pearly ear?
God spoke, and it came out to hear.

Where did you get those arms and hands?
Love made itself into bonds and bands.

Feet, whence did you come, you
   darling things?
From the same box as the cherubs' wings.

How did they all just come to be you?
God thought about me, and so I grew.

But how did you come to us, you dear?
God thought about you, and so
   I am here.

                — *George Macdonald*

I Found God

Sophisticated, worldly-wise,
I searched for God and found
   Him not,
Until one day, the world forgot,
I found Him in my baby's eyes.

—Mary Afton Thacker

"And whoever welcomes a little child
like this in My name welcomes Me."

Matthew 18:5 (NIV)

Children are the hands by which we
take hold of heaven.

—Henry Ward Beecher

"See that you do not look down on
one of these little ones. For I tell you
that their angels in heaven always see
the face of My Father in heaven."

Matthew 18:10,11 (NIV)

Whenever a Little Child Is Born

Whenever a little child is born,
All night long a soft wind rocks the corn;
One more buttercup wakes to the morn,
Somewhere, somewhere.

One more rosebud shy will unfold,
One more grass-blade push
   through the mold,
One more bird-song the air will hold,
Somewhere, somewhere.

                —*Agnes Carter Mason*

The smallest children are nearest to God,
as the smallest planets are nearest the sun.

— *Jean Paul Richter*

Only a Baby Small

Only a baby small,
Dropped from the skies,
Only a laughing face,
Two sunny eyes;
Only two cherry lips,
One chubby nose;
Only two little hands,
Ten little toes.

Only a tender flower
Sent us to rear;
Only a life to love
While we are here;
Only a baby small,
Never at rest;
Small, but how dear to us,
God knoweth best.

—Matthias Barr

You Are More Blessed

You are more blessed
    than other babies are:
Your shining eyes
    grow brighter every day
With radiance that reminds me
    of the star
That showed where Jesus lay.

I like to think that you
    are set apart,
A flower that never sprang
    from earthly loam,
A rose of Heaven that nestles
    in my heart
And dreams about its home.

                —Aline Kilmer

A RADIANT HOPE

A Baby Is a Blessing

A baby is a blessing—
It's a joy to watch it grow,
To see its little toothless smile
And count each tiny toe.

A baby is a blessing,
For its life is bright and new;
Just by being here it gives
Our lives new purpose, too.

A baby is a blessing,
For when faith or hope is gone,
A baby clearly signifies
God's wish that life go on.

—Jill Wolf

Every child comes into the world
with the message that God does
not yet despair of man.

—*Rabindranath Tagore*

. . . one has need of children to
keep one's faith clear and one's
hope bright.

—*Oscar W. Firkins*

I have often thought what a
melancholy world this would be
without children . . .

—*Samuel Taylor Coleridge*

A baby is God's opinion that
life should go on.

— *Carl Sandburg*

Babies are necessary to grown-ups. A new baby is like the beginning of all things— wonder, hope, a dream of possibilities. In a world that is cutting down its trees to build highways, losing its earth to concrete . . . babies are almost the only remaining link with nature, with the natural world of living things from which we spring.

—Eda J. Le Shan

Something to live for came to the place,
Something to die for maybe,
Something to give even sorrow a grace,
And yet it was only a baby!

—Harriet Spofford

Baby darling, wake and see,
Morning's here, my little rose;
Open eyes and smile at me
Ere I clasp and kiss you close.
Baby darling, smile! for then
Mother sees the sun again.

— *Edith Nesbit*

When from the wearying war of life
I seek release,
I look into my Baby's face,
And there find peace.

— *Martha Foote Crow*

Of all the joys that brighten suffering earth,
what joy is welcomed like a newborn child?

— *Caroline Norton*

Keeping Us Young

Children are the most wholesome part of the race, the sweetest, for they are freshest from the hand of God. Whimsical, ingenious, mischievous, they fill the world with joy and good humor. We adults live a life of apprehension as to what they will think of us; a life of defense against their terrifying energy; a life of hard work to live up to their great expectations. We put them to bed with a sense of relief—and greet them in the morning with delight and anticipation. We envy them the freshness of adventure and the discovery of life. In all these ways, children add to the wonder of being alive. In all these ways, they help to keep us young.

—Herbert Hoover

Somewhere the Child

Among the thousands of tiny things growing up all over the land . . . among them somewhere is the child who will write the novel that will stir men's hearts to nobler issues and incite them to better deeds. There is the child who will paint the greatest picture or carve the greatest statue of the age . . .

It may be that I shall preserve one of these children to the race. It is a peg big enough on which to hang a hope, for every child born into the world is a new incarnate thought of God, an ever fresh and radiant possibility.

—Kate Douglas Wiggin

In praising or loving a child, we love and praise not that which is, but that which we hope for.

—*Johann Wolfgang von Goethe*

The potential possibilities of any child are the most intriguing and stimulating in all creation.

—*Ray Lyman Wilbur*

There is no finer investment for any community than putting milk into babies.

—*Winston Churchill*

Among the three or four million cradles now rocking in the land are some which this nation would preserve for ages as sacred things, if we could know which ones they are.

—*Mark Twain*

Every baby born into the world is a finer
one than the last.

— *Charles Dickens*

The Most Marvelous Invention

Never will a time come when the most marvelous recent invention is as marvelous as a newborn baby. The finest of our precision watches, the most supercolossal of our supercargo planes, don't compare with a newborn baby in the number and ingenuity of coils and springs, in the flow and change of chemical solutions, in timing devices and interrelated parts that are irreplaceable.

— *Carl Sandburg*

The Greatest Forces

When God wants a great work done in the world or a great wrong righted, He goes about it in a very unusual way. He doesn't stir up His earthquakes or send forth His thunderbolts. Instead, He has a helpless baby born, perhaps in a simple home and of some obscure mother. And then God puts the idea into the mother's heart, and she puts it into the baby's mind. And then God waits. The greatest forces in the world are not the earthquakes and the thunderbolts. The greatest forces in the world are babies.

—*E. T. Sullivan*

Gladdening the Earth

God sends children for another purpose
than merely to keep up the race—to
enlarge our hearts; and to make us
unselfish and full of kindly sympathies
and affections; to give our souls higher
aims; to call out all our faculties to ex-
tended enterprise and exertion; and to
bring round our firesides bright faces,
happy smiles, and loving, tender hearts.
My soul blesses the great Father, every
day, that He has gladdened the earth
with little children.

— *Mary Botham Howitt*

The parents exist to teach the child, but also they must learn what the child has to teach them; and the child has a very great deal to teach them.

—Arnold Bennett

. . . what instruction does the babe bring to the mother!

—Thomas Wentworth Higginson

Children are God's apostles, sent forth, day by day, to preach of love, and hope and peace.

—James Russell Lowell

We need love's tender lessons taught
As only weakness can;
God hath His small interpreters;
The child must teach the man.

—John Greenleaf Whittier

A babe in a house is a well-spring of pleasure, a
messenger of peace and love, a resting place for
innocence on earth, a link between angels and men.

—Martin F. Tupper

Good News of Great Joy

So Joseph also went up from the town of Nazareth in Galilee to Judea, to Bethlehem the town of David, because he belonged to the house and line of David. He went there to register with Mary, who was pledged to be married to him and was expecting a child. While they were there, the time came for the baby to be born, and she gave birth to her firstborn, a son. She wrapped Him in cloths and placed Him in a manger, because there was no room for them in the inn.

And there were shepherds living out in the fields nearby, keeping watch over their flocks at night. An angel of the Lord appeared to them, and the glory of the Lord shone around them, and they were terrified. But the angel said to them, "Do not be afraid. I bring you good news of great joy that will be for all the people. Today in the town of David a Savior has been born to you; He is Christ the Lord. This will be a sign to you: You will find a baby wrapped in cloths and lying in a manger."

Suddenly a great company of the heavenly host appeared with the angel, praising God and saying, "Glory to God in the highest, and on earth peace to men on whom His favor rests."

When the angels had left them and gone into heaven, the shepherds said to one another, "Let's go to Bethlehem and see this thing that has happened, which the Lord has told us about."

So they hurried off and found Mary and Joseph, and the baby, who was lying in the manger. When they had seen Him, they spread the word concerning what had been told them about this child, and all who heard it were amazed at what the shepherds said to them. But Mary treasured up all these things and pondered them in her heart.

Luke 2:4-19 (NIV)

Baby's First Christmas

On baby's first Christmas
There's a beautiful tree
With many bright colors
For baby to see.
Along baby's crib
Bells that jingle are strung,
And close by the chimney
Baby's stocking is hung.

On baby's first Christmas
There's wonderful joy
In giving to baby
That first special toy—
A ball or a rattle,
A soft teddy bear
That baby will cuddle
And take everywhere.

On baby's first Christmas
It's easy to find
That one tiny child
Brings another to mind,
For baby reminds us
In a tangible way
That Jesus was born
On that first Christmas day.

—Jill Wolf

LOVE'S REWARD

A mother's pride, a father's joy.

— Sir Walter Scott

If you ever become a father, I think the strangest and strongest sensation of your life will be hearing for the first time the thin cry of your own child. For a moment you have the strange feeling of being double, but there is something more, quite impossible to analyze—perhaps the echo in a man's heart of all the sensations felt by all the fathers and mothers . . . at a similar instant in the past. It is a very tender, but also a very ghostly feeling.

— Lafcadio Hearn

No man can possibly know what life means, what the world means, what anything means, until he has a child and loves it. And then the whole universe changes and nothing will ever again seem exactly as it seemed before.

— Lafcadio Hearn

"A woman giving birth to a child has pain because her time has come; but when her baby is born she forgets the anguish because of her joy that a child is born into the world."

John 16:21 (NIV)

The coarsest father gains a new impulse to labor from the moment of his baby's birth. Every stroke he strikes is for his child. New social aims, and new moral motives come vaguely up to him.

—Thomas Wentworth Higginson

Generations

When one becomes a father, then first one becomes a son. Standing by the crib of one's own baby, with that world-old pang of compassion and protectiveness toward this so little creature that has all its course to run, the heart flies back in yearning and gratitude to those who felt just so towards one's self. Then for the first time one understands the homely succession of sacrifices and pains by which life is transmitted and fostered down the stumbling generations of men.

— *Christopher Morley*

Mrs. Lofty keeps a carriage,
So do I;
She has dappled grays to draw it,
None have I;
She's no prouder with her coachman
Than am I
With my blue-eyed, laughing baby
Trundling by.

—*Mrs. C. Gildersleeve (Longstreet)*

You are the trip I did not take;
You are the pearls I cannot buy;
You are my blue Italian lake;
You are my piece of foreign sky.

—*Anne Campbell*

I love these little people; and it is not a slight thing,
when they, who are so fresh from God, love us.

— Charles Dickens

Give a little love to a child, and you get a great deal back.

— John Ruskin

A child enters your home and makes so much noise for twenty years that you can hardly stand it: then departs leaving the house so silent that you think you will go mad.

— John Andrew Holmes

LIKE A ROSE

A sweet new blossom of humanity,
fresh fallen from God's own home,
to flower on earth.

— Gerald Massey

A rose with all its sweetest leaves
yet folded.

— Lord Byron

Sweetest li'l' feller, everybody knows;
Dunno what to call him, but he's
    mighty lak' a rose.

— Frank L. Stanton

Little Hands

Soft little hands that stray and clutch,
Like fern fronds curl and uncurl bold,
While baby faces lie in such
Close sleep as flowers at night
   that fold,
What is it you would clasp and hold,
Wandering outstretched
   with wilful touch?
O fingers small of shell-tipped rose,
How should you know you hold
   so much?
Two full hearts beating you inclose,
Hopes, fears, prayers, longings,
   joys and woes,—
All yours to hold, O little hands!
More, more than wisdom understands
And love, love only knows.

                —Laurence Binyon

The world has no such flower in any land,
And no such pearl in any gulf the sea,
As any babe on any mother's knee.

—*Algernon Swinburne*

Étude Realiste

I

A baby's feet, like seashells pink,
Might tempt, should heaven see meet,
An angel's lips to kiss, we think,
A baby's feet.

Like rose-hued sea-flowers
    toward the heat
They stretch and spread and wink
Their ten soft buds that part and meet.

No flower-bells that expand and shrink
Gleam half so heavenly sweet,
As shine on life's untrodden brink
A baby's feet.

II

A baby's hands, like rosebuds furled,
Where yet no leaf expands,
Ope if you touch, though close
    upcurled,—
A baby's hands.

Then, even as warriors grip their brands
When battle's bolt is hurled,
They close, clenched hard
    like tightening bands.

No rosebuds yet by dawn impearled
Match, even in loveliest lands,
The sweetest flowers in all the world,—
A baby's hands.

—Algernon Swinburne

Counting Baby's Toes

Dear little bare feet, dimpled and white,
In your long nightgown wrapped for
    the night;
Come, let me count all your
    queer little toes,
Pink as the heart of a shell or a rose.

One is a lady that sits in the sun;
Two is a baby, and *three* is a nun;
Four is a lily with innocent breast;
Five is a birdie asleep in its nest.

                  —*Author Unknown*

Then there had been the inspection
of their child from head to toe as
he watched Annie undress the baby
before bedtime. The tiny perfect
fingernails and toenails astonished
him the most. There were like the
small pink shells you scuffed up in
the sands of tropical beaches, he
whispered, counting them.

— *Kathryn Hulme*

First Footsteps

A little way, more soft and sweet
Than fields aflower with May,
A babe's feet, venturing,
  scarce complete
A little way.

Eyes full of dawning day
Look up for mother's eyes to meet,
Too blithe for song to say.

Glad as the golden spring to greet
It first live leaflet's play,
Love, laughing, leads the little feet
A little way.

—Algernon Swinburne

Tucking the Baby In

The dark-fringed eyelids slowly close
On eyes serene and deep;
Upon my breast my own sweet child
Has gently dropped to sleep;
I kiss his soft and dimpled cheek,
I kiss his rounded chin,
Then lay him on his little bed,
And tuck my baby in.

How fair and innocent he lies;
Like some small angel strayed,
His face still warmed
    by God's own smile,
That slumbers unafraid;
Or like some new embodied soul,
Still pure from taint of sin—
My thoughts are reverent as I stoop
To tuck my baby in.

O what am I that I should train
An angel for the skies;
Or mix the patent draught that feeds
The soul within those eyes?
I reach him up to the sinless Hands
Before his cares begin,—
Great Father, with Thy folds of love,
O tuck my baby in.

— Curtis May